I Am Both Woman and Child, Both Tame and Wild

A Collection of Poems, Illustrations, and Reflections

MAGGIE MAZE

AuthorHouse™
1663 Liberty Drive
Bloomington, IN 47403
www.authorhouse.com
Phone: 1 (833) 262-8899

ISBN: 978-1-6655-0535-2 (sc)
ISBN: 978-1-6655-0536-9 (hc)
ISBN: 978-1-6655-0534-5 (e)

Library of Congress Control Number: 2020920955

Print information available on the last page.

Published by AuthorHouse 07/11/2022

authorHOUSE

In memory of my parents,
Bud and Marg,
who made this book possible by
believing in me with their love and support.

Thank you, Mom and Dad.

For Dane, Alexander, and Caitlin,
and for my grandchildren,
Sailor, River, Riley, and Claire.

Contents

Part 1 Illustrations with Poems 1

It's Margarita Time! 3

Sci-Fi Electric Babe 4

Feel the Music 6

A Pose among Hillside Flowers 8

Venus Rapture 11

Girl Power 13

Birds of a Feather 14

Treasure Love 17

Breezes 18

Autumn Park Bench 20

A Portrait of Seven Daughters 22

Happy Sunshine Sister Friends 24

Seven Sister Bumblebees 26

Valentine Via 28

Celtic Lass 30

Lovely Bride-to-Be 32

Trick or Treat 34

Bewitched Witch 36

It Had to Be You 38

Catch: I Cast upon Thee a Haunted Halloween! 40

Get Your Witch On! 42

Hauntingly Sweet Witch Trio 45

Afternoon Holiday Tea 46

Outdoor Christmas Fun 48

Holiday Cheers 51

Ladies' Outdoor Luncheon 52

Part 2 Greeting Card Illustrations 54

Engaging with Nature 57
It's Margarita Time! 58
Dancing Flowers 60
Like the Sun's Rays 63
Dancing Stars 64
God bless America! 66
Catch! 68

Valentine's Day 70

Fabric of Love 72
Surround Hearts..74
Sending My Love 75
My Three Lovely Granddaughters...76
Sweets and Treats...77
Heart Pillow Message..78
Butterfly Kisses...80
Puppy Love 81

St. Patrick's Day 82

Catch!...84
With Irish Charms..86
Irish upon a Star 88
Luck o' the Irish t'ye! 90
Happy St. Patrick's Day!...91

Easter 92
Bunny Belle 93
Easter Eggs 94
Easter Basket 95
Somebunny Loves You! 96

Halloween 97
Masked Witch: Scare and Beware 101
Under Your Spell 105

Thanksgiving 106
Gobble Wobble Turkey 107
Thanksgiving Blessings 108
Count Your Blessings 109
Thanksgiving Scarecrow 110

Christmas 111
A Very Merry Doggie 112
Catch: The Spirit of Christmas 113
Catch 114
Christmas Candle 116
Friends and Family 118
Christmas Wrap 120
Seductive Christmas Ornament 122
Santa's Present 123

Kokopelli Twin Designs 124

Part 3   Poems and Reflections 127

My Studio 128
A Morning Dream Surrenders 129
Love Slumbers 130
Lovers Be At Once 131
I Suppose, ...132
I Am 133
Passionless 135
2020 Pandemic: Days of Uncertainty 137
The Annual Midnight Ball 139
The *Hot* Bartender 140
Reflections: The Joy of Love 142
My Dear Friend Noel 145

Part 4   Fashion and Style 148

Today's Woman: A Study in Style 149
Metro Riverside 150
Afro-American Style 154
Coat Chic 155
Purses and Boots 156

Part 5   Black-and-White Samples 157

Basket o' Kittens 158
Scarecrow 159
Autumn Park Bench 160
Boo Crew 161
It Had to Be You (Halloween Witch) 162
Ladies' Outdoor Luncheon 163
Outdoor Christmas Fun 164
Snow Family 165

Part 1

Illustrations with Poems

It's Margarita Time!

It's margarita time!
You bring the salt;
I'll supply the lime.
It's a perfect date
of a citrus sour mix
and a tequila first-rate.
Goblets full to the rim,
ice crushed or on the rocks,
a paper straw the final trim.
Life is short, so indulge we must,
sipping and conversing,
wet lips coated a salty dust.
Let's make a festive toast:
All should enjoy a margarita
From coast to coast.

Sci-Fi Electric Babe

Sci-fi cool and totally hot,
her apparel says quite a lot.
She's bound by electric volts,
connected by wires and various bolts.

She's often the subject of a Google search,
always maintaining her anonymous perch.
Her followers seek a specific sign,
but nothing relevant appears online.

She's versed in a secret virtual trade
where there's strange magic to be made.
Is she for real or putting on a show?
Perhaps the world will never know.

Feel the Music

Feel the music,
close your eyes;
let it vibrate through your being.
Imagine a sensory paradise
of melodic sounds
pulsating and cajoling—
a serene, rhythmic flow.
At times both calm and stirring.
You move in tandem
in realms both seen and unseen.
You are the instruments
and the receiver
in the music of life.

A Pose among Hillside Flowers

My lover suggested a casual stroll,
The day invitingly warm and sunny bright,
To share a blanket picnic and meadow roll.
His allure induced my passion's delight.

We listened quietly along the way
Amid sweet aromas filling the gentle air
As nearby crickets chirped to say,
Welcome to nature's secret lair.

Upon a clearing of colorful flowers,
We nestled near a secluded hill.
Surrounded by his masculine powers,
The earth moved, yet all was still.

My lover encouraged me to pose,
Whispered, "You're a beautiful sight."
Declared his love from head to toes
Till day spun into a starry night.

Venus Rapture

Wrapped in passion,
Venus rapture entices.
A bird of paradise
captures her dreams,
weaving them into
spiritual bliss.
Her earthly contours
beckon beyond mere gaze.
She reflects
internal peace in love.

© 2010 MMD

Girl Power

In body and mind,
We are strong and kind.
We girls possess strength
And will go the length.
We have a purpose and will find our way
Through the thick and thin of every day.
We succeed in handling numerous tasks,
All the while wearing many kinds of masks.
Do not doubt what we can achieve.
"The sky's the limit" is the motto we believe.
We won't back down; we're here to stay.
From our convictions we do not stray.
We love and support those we love.
Our passions guide us with faith from above.
While we are many and quite a few,
Our objectives are similar and anew.
Appearing different but of the same tribe,
We're quite impossible to describe.
Since I'm one and giving my best shot,
Here's to girl power and our lot!

Birds of a Feather

As days have turned into years,
We have remained two birds of a feather.
We've shared laughter and tears
And fared well in all relationship weather.

We have taken to the skies in flight
On wings of love from the very start.
We've managed not to lose sight
Of what matters most in our hearts.

Our young have flown from their nest,
And we've sung many a life's sweet song.
Our trials and patience have been put to the test,
Yet we've endured; this is where we belong.

Oh! Such a wild pair of colorful birds are we,
Soaring through heavenly skies together.
Yet settled in our ways in our own family tree,
We'll always be two birds of a feather!

© 2012 MMD

Treasure Love

All sea creatures gather round.
There's valuable treasure to be found.
It is not jewels, coins, or gold,
And cannot be traded, bought, or sold.

Where the sea meets the sandy shore,
Crustaceans comb the ocean floor.
Each creature's instinct knows
Treasure love's true meaning flows.

My mermaid soul swims in search
From the beginning of time at birth,
Diving coral reefs from above
For everlasting treasure love.

Treasure love brings beauty to life,
Soothes the soul in midst of strife,
Breathes life to heart's eternal beat,
And melts away hate with its heat.

Breezes

When I think of you,
warm breezes envelop my being,
bringing me closer to you.

©2019MMD

Autumn Park Bench

Late summer wafts
ease, a cool autumn breeze
bringing vibrant colors upon
varied kinds of leaves.

A curious birdie perched,
taking a rest from flight
amid autumn's splendid art.
Oh! Such an amazing sight!

Swaying trees whisper
a soothing autumn song.
Come, delight in nature's magic;
it's where you belong.

A Portrait of Seven Daughters

A beautiful, fragrant spring day
is perfect for a backyard game or play.
But Mother has arranged for a photo shoot,
and Father agrees to it without a hoot.

It'll be a portrait of us seven girls
with hair styled straight or in curls.
We're dressed in the latest Victorian style,
fidgeting and chatting all the while.

The photographer is certainly put to the test;
after all, he must present the very best.
Persuading us girls to sit still and smile
can be an enormous and challenging trial.

Finally we settle down and put on a happy face,
knowing our parents are content in their place.
This special portrait shall last for years and years,
bringing memories forth of fun and happy tears.

Happy Sunshine Sister Friends

Happy sunshine sister friends are we!
We share secrets and our favorite things,
helping each other climb our backyard tree,
playing outside and swinging on swings.

Our favorite kitty cat, named Shadow,
follows us on adventures everywhere we go,
exploring nearby hillside meadows
in weather fair or when wind blows.

Caring and sharing and so much more,
we're happy sister friends to the core!

Seven Sister Bumblebees

Seven sister bumblebees buzzing around,
all buzzing a story about their family hive.
Through uncertain climate, they have found
working together is necessary to survive.
Their sisterhood stands on solid ground
as all seven are buzzing, happy to be alive.

(Climate change theme)

Valentine Via

To be around
Via is such a treat.
She's so naturally cute,
at times funny,
and always so sweet.

Her hugs and kisses
are given with adorable care.
Oh, sweet, darling Via,
such joy and love
you possess to share!

©2020MMD

Celtic Lass

She's no ordinary Irish lass
perched upon a shamrock garden;
she possesses a certain Irish class
but expects no special pardon.

Dressed in the finest silk, velvet, and plaid,
she's a sight of breathtaking beauty and style.
All eyes upon her from many an Irish lad,
they present sincere devotion all the while.

She raises her fine Waterford goblet
filled with a savory, golden lager beer.
Admired near and afar among the Celtic set,
she's ready to propose a toast and cheer.

She exclaims, "Happy St. Patrick's Day!
Lest we forget those have gone before
who set the path along the Irish way,
may we always remember our Irish lore!"

© 2016MMD

Lovely Bride-to-Be

These three little birdies love to sing
love songs merry upon their wings.
From the highest peak sprinkled with snow
to the deepest canyons far below,
for Corri Ann, lovely bride-to-be,
beautiful, strong, and gentle is she.

Her wedding dress of delicate silk and lace
shall be adorned with care and spiritual grace.
For upon her approaching wedding day,
those two devoted words, "I do," she'll say.

She possesses a true and tender love
with God's blessing from above.
Desires her family and friends to see,
her tender love for her husband-to-be.

Lucky and elated are we
as she'll soon join our family tree.

Trick or Treat

Trick or treat
in snow, rain, or sleet.
Creepy ghosts and goblins abound
in darkened alleys around town.

It only comes once a year,
when mere mortals show their fear.
So do your very best to scare;
look over your shoulder and beware.

You'll know you are not alone
when eerie noises chill your bones.
So grin wide and be upbeat
as you cry, "Trick or treat!"

TRICK or TREAT

©2009MMD

Bewitched Witch

Everything twitched
when this Halloween witch
turned on the switch,
sending unwelcome spells
from dark, evil wells,
causing chaos across nearby hills,
giving local residents eerie chills.

Flapping vampire bats filled the night,
erasing what was left of the moonlight,
releasing a torrent of awful plight
to all who refuse to believe
all is haunted on devils' eve.

It Had to Be You

Of the beguiling, creepy crew,
I knew it had to be you.
With a blink of your inviting azure eyes,
a bat appeared from moonlit, luminescent skies.
Perhaps it was simply a notion,
perceived from mutual sensuous motion.
So without hesitation you cast a spell
upon the body and soul where I dwell.
Appeared before me a goblet of love potion;
it looked like webs of silken desire mixed
with love's bottomless ocean.
I drank swiftly with a thirst I never knew before.
The mysterious potion warmed and then melted my inner core,
affecting and stirring my being, leaving me wanting much more.
At once, then I knew.
It had to be you.

Catch: I Cast upon Thee a Haunted Halloween!

Oh, such a haunting Halloween!
One that you've never seen.
That this witch casts an unknown spell
Is beyond scary; all is not well.

A witch of pimples, warts, and much more,
she feeds on others' hype and folklore.
Wrapped in the latest eerie couture,
ready to seize you, I can assure.

There may be nothing quite worse
than having her toss you an unwanted curse.
Only you will know if it's bad or good,
so heed your trek in the neighborhood.

This moonlit night is totally surreal.
To you, mere mortal, I do appeal,
extend well wishes on this creepy night,
keep all safe and away from fright.

This Halloween witch is out to scare
acquaintances and strangers everywhere.
From houses, dens, and the nearby lair,
"Happy Halloween" to you, I do declare.

© 2017 MMD

Get Your Witch On!

As Halloween draws near,
remember there is much to fear.
From creeping spiders and eerie ghosts
to possessed zombies and evil hosts.

A witch of unlimited evil source,
she lacks reason with no remorse.
Spooky bats follow her everywhere,
from alleys, streets, and the nearby lair.

Swathed in the latest eerie attire,
her look can't hide a burning desire
to wreak havoc on all seen and unseen,
from old souls to babies to preteens.

Drifting across the eve's unbeaten path,
casting spells of unwanted wrath
upon those that fail to believe.
Beware of all on this haunting eve.

Happy Halloween!

© 2017 MMD

Hauntingly Sweet Witch Trio

Sweet and sassy, three witches are we,
seeking to scare all that be.
This Halloween night of moonlit glow,
come creatures from above and far below.
Creeping spiders and eerie ghosts
to possessed pumpkins and evil hosts.

Sly and sneaky, three witches are we,
seeking to seize all that remain free.
Drifting across the night's unbeaten path,
casting spells of unwelcome wrath
upon those that fail to believe.
Beware of all on this haunting eve.
Darling and daring, three witches are we—
known as witches Trix, Ava, and Cassie—
we exclaim to all seen and unseen,
from aging seniors to babies to preteens,
"Trick or treat," this Halloween night!
This eve shall fade till next year's light.

Afternoon Holiday Tea

Teapot aromas summon a playful cast.
There's an owl named Who and Daisy Clown,
with friends from afar and of the past.
All have arrived to sip the best brew in town.

The table is set for my friends and me.
There's sweet honey jam and lemon cake.
Chatting over cups of warm holiday tea,
oh, such fun, lifelong memories we make!

All are welcome to tea this afternoon,
bringing happy stories of tea party lore
while sounds of sipping all but a tune.
Tea is plentiful, so help yourself to more.

Outdoor Christmas Fun

All is still before winter's sleep.
Snow has fallen and is quite deep.
Time to decorate and play outside,
the landscape white, far and wide.

The season's offerings are finally here,
bringing forth much Christmas cheer.
Paint your cheeks a merry glow;
there's fun to be had in the snow!

There's plenty to do and see,
from wrapping red bows on many a tree
to building the biggest snowman in town
and sledding the steepest hill around.

There are snow angels to be made
while listening to carolers on parade.
Christmas songs echo down the street
as neighbors gather to chat and meet.

Start your play at morning's light.
Be sure your mittens fit just right.
Winter outdoors is so much fun,
come indulge till the season's done.

Merry Christmas

© 2016 MMD

© 2009 MaggieMazeDesign

Holiday Cheers

How the merry season lends
to visiting with the best of friends.
Twinkling, colored holiday lights
bring much-needed and festive nights.

Soothe stressed and busy minds
with delicious drinks of all kinds.
There's spiced tea, wine, and beer
to encourage much holiday cheer.

It's fun to catch up on all anew
as the days to visit are all but a few.
Everyone has an exciting story to tell;
on no one's lips does a secret dwell.

Let's make a special holiday toast,
so everyone can hear from coast to coast.
"Bless all who happen upon this day,
with peace and prosperity every day!"

Part 2

Greeting Card Illustrations

Engaging with Nature

Refreshing to the toes.
Soothing to the spirit.
Renewing to the mind.
Calming to the senses.

It's Margarita Time!

When you're in my company,
you're in Margaritaville!

Dancing Flowers

May
colorful showers
bring dancing flowers
of happiness
to your day!

Like the Sun's Rays

Like the sun's rays,
I can feel you all over me,
from head to toe.

Dancing Stars

May dancing stars
rock
your universe!

Shine on!

God bless America!

God Bless America!

©2018MMD

Catch!

Tossing birthday wishes
your way
for a sweet 'n' fancy
fun-filled day!

© 2015 MMD

Valentine's Day

Happy Valentine's Day!

Fabric of Love

May many textured
fabrics of love
embrace you always.

Surround Hearts

On this Valentine's Day
may you be surrounded by
sweets, treats, and loving hearts.

Sending My Love

On this Valentine's Day,
whether you're with me or away,
I am with you in a loving, spiritual way
from morning throughout the day.

Happy Valentine's Day to my love!

© 2017 MMD

My Three Lovely Granddaughters

My three lovely granddaughters,
dressed in fancy Victorian couture,
bring warm and cheerful smiles
across vast chilly and frozen miles.

Adorned with hearts galore,
full of sweetness and so much more,
sending happiness and love your way
on this Valentine's Day!

Sweets and Treats

Of all the sweets and treats
this Valentine's Day,
you're the sweetest by far!

Happy Valentine's Day!

Heart Pillow Message

This heart-shaped pillow,
soft, cuddly, and scarlet red,
is filled with hugs and kisses
to keep you loved all day long,
from dawn's rise till dusk's bed.

Happy Valentine's Day, my love!

© 2012 MMD

Butterfly Kisses

Sending butterfly kisses
and warm embraces ...

Happy Valentine's Day!

Puppy Love

Hoping your Valentine's Day
is a heap of sweet Valentine wishes
and wet doggie kisses.

St. Patrick's Day

Irish Cheers!

Catch!

Tossing shamrocks your way
for a happy St. Patrick's Day!

© 2015 MMD

With Irish Charms

May the luck of the Irish
be with you always!

Happy St. Patrick's Day!

Irish upon a Star

© 2015 MMD

Irish upon a star ...
You're my lucky charm!

Happy St. Patrick's Day!

Luck o' the Irish t'ye!

Happy St. Patrick's Day!

Easter

Bunny Belle

Bunny Belle is hatching
an "egg-stra" special
Easter for you.

Easter Eggs

Hatching sweet Easter wishes your way
for a fun and delightful Easter day.

Easter Basket

Snowball, my pet bunny, has much to say
on this beautiful springtime Easter day.
Bringing warmth and renewal to nature's sleep
in a garden of colored eggs for you to keep.
Snowball's gifts from over and above
to you, this Easter basket full of love.

Somebunny Loves You!

Halloween

When Halloween comes around,
a headless zombie can be found
sipping a favorite blood-red drink,
arousing fear to all who think.

She appeared without a head,
leading onlookers to totally dread.
Her apparent objective to scare away
all who approach on Halloween day.

Happy haunting Halloween!

No need to lose your head.
It's only Halloween!

Masked Witch: Scare and Beware

Boo Crew

Under Your Spell

Thanksgiving

Gobble Wobble Turkey

Thanksgiving Blessings

Count Your Blessings

Thanksgiving Scarecrow

Christmas

A Very Merry Doggie

Doggone it!
Have a very merry Christmas!

Catch: The Spirit of Christmas

Catch ...

The joyful spirit
of Christmas,
and pass it on!

Catch . . .

© 2014 MMD

Christmas Candle

May this Christmas candle
bring you happiness, good health, and prosperity
now and throughout the new year!

© 2016 MMD

Friends and Family

'Tis the season to celebrate friends and family,
Sharing and caring.

May the Christmas spirit be with you always.

Christmas Wrap

May this Christmas season
wrap you in warmth,
contentment, and love.

©2018MMD

Seductive Christmas Ornament

Affectionate Christmas kisses
await you under the mistletoe.

© 2011 MMD

Santa's Present

Dear Santa Claus,
You top the list of gifts I've asked for this year.
Let's unwrap the night!

Kokopelli

From the North American Southwest

Kokopelli is mostly known throughout the four-corner states

of the southwest as a traveling musician, trader of goods, and

lover of women. His reputation includes
being a master of fertility.

I see Kokopelli as a fun guy, someone I'd like to
hang out with if he were here today. He's optimistic,
outgoing, carefree, and funny. And he possesses
animal magnetism. He loves to flirt and plays the flute
to woo women. Kokopelli never has a bad hair day.

I hope you enjoy him as much as I do.

Part 3

Poems and Reflections

My Studio

My studio,
A place of stirrings, imagination, and creativity
from which daydreaming encounters surface.
It's the idle mind that seeks to integrate passion
into the day's extensions,
thus making the smallest of insignificance
into the greatest of matter.
In this perception
lies a universal thought
only you can determine.

A Morning Dream Surrenders

A morning dream surrenders.
Daylight delights into eternal, enchanted evenings.
Sweet passion inspires,
singing sensuous breezes
around love's earthly contours.
The winds of desire
carry searching hearts
to become shining stars falling into one another.

Love Slumbers

Love slumbers in heaven's depth,
awaiting to be reawakened.
The morning's first rays
penetrate yearnings only known in love.
The dawn beckons its horizon.

Lovers Be At Once

Lovers be
at once
or not at all.
Passion ignites
love's flame-burning time.
Distance yields
its fading light.

The stroke of love's hour,
infinite minutes lost.
Passionate memories
remain through the space between,
carrying our dancing thoughts of desire
to be at once
lovers,
or not at all.

I Suppose,

I suppose at the very least,
the elusive, fragmented course
by which you travel
away from me
brings to me
inspiration
to create that which I seek.
Unable to grasp,
my heart strives
to understand
but cannot
as only the mind can.
The heart listens ...

I Am

I am
Both woman and child,
Both tame and wild.
I am
Many things seen and unseen,
And of realms in-between.
I am
A vessel full of love,
Of spiritual grace from above.
I am
A verse etched in stone.
In eternity I am not alone.
I am

A breath of fresh air
To comfort and share.
I am
A dancing flower in the breeze.
A songbird chirping in the trees.
I am
All that I am meant to be
And much more than just me.

Passionless

For he is not
but consumed of himself
in mirror's imagery.
Self-gratification rules,
clueless but safe.
Deceit desires
a facade for
failure in passion.
His interests swell,
material objects,
His love dwells
nowhere.
She remains

a blur, a fog,
textbook worthy.
Declares affection,
is clingy,
kiss like mother,
touch minimal—a pet.
Human nature cools,
maternal blame.
Succumb to passionlessness.
My grave deepens.
No sound of music.
Withering, weak,
contagious source,
becoming you—
a prop
to be desired.
Light fades.
Mirror knows
only you
in yours alone.

2020 Pandemic: Days of Uncertainty

Oh, how the pandemic does overwhelm,
steering my fears and anxious thoughts.
Like a sinking boat without a helm,
a calm, safe cove is purposely sought.

It's an invisible yet contagious foe.
Only isolation can provide a safety net,
bringing along many an uninvited woe
of having needs no longer met.

I lay pensive and slow-moving
as the world turns another day.
One can find limited soothing,
managing one's safe way.

Streets and stores are bare.
Only those deemed essential stir.
Masked faces, lonely eyes do stare,
missing their towns' constant whir.

All lives are affected; no one is exempt.
Health care workers tend to the sick.
Dressed in PPE, they shall not tempt
as COVID-19 is scary, hard to predict.

I follow the guidelines put in place.
My survival is the fate I choose.
Wash my hands, cover my face,
out in public there is much to lose.

At times it seems all is lost.
The pandemic always on the move,
ruining livelihoods at all cost.
It has absolutely nothing to prove.

The Annual Midnight Ball

'Tis the season to cherish and recall
Past galas and the annual Midnight Ball.
All shall travel from far and near
Since the events come just once a year.

Partners bursting with anticipated desire
Have only one whom they admire.
Pretty young ladies await their place,
Dressed in the finest satin and lace.

Gentlemen stand poised amid the room,
sensing the ladies' sensual perfume.
They summon their partners with exuded charm
to dance the night away, arm in arm.

Once their ladies' love is upon their wings,
how the gentlemen's hearts do merrily sing.
The years collect, but all shall cherish
knowing evenings like this shall ne'er perish.

The *Hot* Bartender

The bar, dimly lit and very cool.
I took a seat on a leather stool.
The bartender inquired my choice of drink.
He smiled and gave me a flirty wink.

He poured me a double scotch,
clearly a drink he could not botch.
Like liquor he was ever so smooth.
Oh, how his testosterone did ooze!

He stood tall at six feet two,
With eyes a deep sea-aqua blue.
His hair blond in a man bun,
golden tresses perfectly spun.

His voice, confident and quite deep,
conversing with the help and barkeep.
Making drinks with precision and flair,
seemingly above any stress or wear.

He moved swiftly behind the bar
with a physical presence way above par.
My eyes wandered to his tight jeans;
he was an Adonis by all means.

All the female waitstaff wanted him,
perhaps to date or a quickie on a whim.
I, too, couldn't help but admire
how he ignited my deepest desire.

I found myself on fire and in a trance,
wondering, *Is there even a slight chance?*
I'd have to give it my best shot,
As this bartender is totally hot!

Reflections: The Joy of Love

Shine your light of love on.
Feel the warmth of light and love on your face,
from the rays of light reflecting back.
Embrace the moment,
whether brief or vast,
shallow or deep.
Connecting, not alienating.
The moment becomes past.
A pebble of conscious perspective in experience.
Unwrap the present as it is a gift indeed.

Indulge and explore.
Become you in all the possibilities infinite in life and love.
Unleash former boundaries to create an atmosphere of
unknown, unexpected surprises and delights.
This is an exciting concept in consciousness as rewards are
plentiful in the spirit of just being.

Love's universe awaits.
Passion's paradise dreams of sensual bliss.

Oh, hopeless romantic am I.
Yet it yields a power divine in desire and all-consuming.
My search continues, but destiny may be cloaked in disguise.

The journey is a constant struggle, straining in contrast
to the result. If I look too hard, the obvious may render
dissatisfaction, and real attributes become invisible.
A peaceful, less critical objective is required if I am to reach
the unique and genuine place of tranquility in my heart.
I know it is within my grasp. I shall be patient. I have been broken,
but I can heal. Contentment carries me in daily doings.
I am blessed. Love is here. Love is now.

Love's water beckons.
Dive in, soothe my aching, starved heart.
Welcome love's current.
I swim in delight and float on desire.
Contentment flows through me, awakening
waves of energy and truth.
Truth opened the dam.
Oh, most passionate and sensuous lover, know it is not common.
It is rare indeed to feel such enormous attraction,

not unlike sheer magnetism, pulling toward one another,

grasping, longing to connect. Feel the power.

The chemistry cannot be ignored.

To be in your presence is an excitement beyond mere words.

Only you have this beautiful and natural power over me.

You stir me like no other.

Only you possess my heart, soul, and body.

I am yours entirely.

Let us take ourselves to infinite passions,

our senses melting together.

Oh, how you take over me, a seduction like no other.

Hugging, kissing, caressing, we breathe in unison.

Oh, glorious love in intimacy! This is what we were made for.

This is what nourishes our appetite for love.

This fills our capacity to indulge in the best life has to offer.

Desire naked, reflecting the power of love.

My Dear Friend Noel

As I drive along the plain fields of rural earth, cornstalks spread across the vast landscape yielding to the horizon, I acknowledge my roots embedded deep in the mineral-rich soil. A feeling of contentment washes over me; love for and about family beckons my appreciation. Like the harvest ...

As you look mortality in the face, it is difficult to comprehend the inner workings of your current state of mind. Without any further dialogue, I know you've buried any minute evidence of lingering fear and are in a constant state of preparation for what awaits you on the other side. Fear exhibits no foundation as your faith takes you beyond.

Words are but a ripple on the surface of expression, yet they possess a deep dimension of meaningful thought of intention. My intention is to search for the words my heart aches to yield, relevant in our friendship and in celebrating your life being.

Sitting with you on my deck, I gaze over my flowerpots to the pine trees off in the distance. Relaxed and content in the moment,

I indulge a puff of clove and drink an ice-cold IPA beer. "Life is good," falls off my lips to your ears, and you agree with a smile, my dear friend Noel. Peace and love, your signature description, embodied more so than the sum of its parts, is indeed representative of your casual approach to life and authentic demeanor.

In celebration of you, Noel, my fellow mermaid; I give to you heartfelt stirrings from the bonds of friendship that run deep between us. The sweet ribbons of our friendship are parcels of shared moments to be cherished always.

May heaven's current carry you into God's calming waters of eternal peace and everlasting love. May your spirit swim in delight as you gently submerge your earthly contours. Relieving the boundaries that hold ever so tightly, you surrender your fins with fluid abandon.

You are a bright and colorful gift to all who have the good fortune of knowing you.

You decorate the people in your life with an uncommon weave of loyalty and genuine care.

With striking reluctance, I attempt to grasp, with hesitation, a world without your physical presence. An overwhelming sense of loss envelops me and at once fleeting, I realize your strength and spirit persevere in spite of the weight of your daily struggle. Your quiet strength and colorful spirit extinguish the air of loss, filling the space with promise, knowing you shall be at peace. A place we all strive to be.

Because you are loved, the pain you endure is contagious to those who love you. No one is exempt. It's a physical world issue, and how demanding it is indeed. You will always live in my heart and in the hearts of many. Tears of joy for you.

Part 4

Fashion and Style

Today's Woman: A Study in Style

Today's woman—
she exudes confidence in
the way she carries herself
in style without complication.
The look she possesses
may change with a new hairstyle
or with the addition of
a simple accessory.

Today's fashions reflect
the various roles she may play.
Her creative options have
no boundaries.
Today's woman embraces
life in harmony
with herself and her
surroundings.

She is the essence of the new modern
spirit of the millennium.

Metro Riverside

© 2012 MMD

Afro-American Style

Coat Chic

©2009 MMD

Purses and Boots

If I wasn't reading, I'd be shopping!

Part 5

Black-and-White Samples

Basket o' Kittens

Scarecrow

Autumn Park Bench

160

Boo Crew

It Had to Be You (Halloween Witch)

Ladies' Outdoor Luncheon

Outdoor Christmas Fun

Snow Family

Author Biography

 **"Maggie Maze"**, aka Margaret Campbell was born in Detroit, MI and now resides in Howell, MI. A middle child, number 5 of 10 children, she found contentment in drawing, as parental attention was spread out, among her many siblings. After graduating from Marian High School, she attended Eastern Michigan University and went on to study at The Center For Creative Studies in Detroit.

Margaret enjoys and is inspired by fashion which is reflected in many of her illustrations. As both illustrator and writer she presents an image with a brief story or verse. One drawing or "pose" can be changed into numerous themes; from a Halloween illustration to Christmas and then to St. Patrick's Day. Many of her designs have been applied to numerous products including greeting cards, magnets, bookmarks and gift bags with gift tags.

In writing, she expresses various emotions: from a romantic perch, she writes poems of love. One can feel her anxiety in her poem, "Coronavirus; Days of Uncertainty", to her playful side in "The Hot Bartender", and in her poem, "I Am" she attempts to find descriptions of her existential place in the universe. "Passionless", was written about the end of a marriage. All these are reflections of her experiences and yearning, of finding one's place and of just being.

Printed in the United States
by Baker & Taylor Publisher Services